SERENDIPITY

Poems about Love
in High School

Written By
Alina Gonzalez

With Illustrations by
Caitlyn Simons

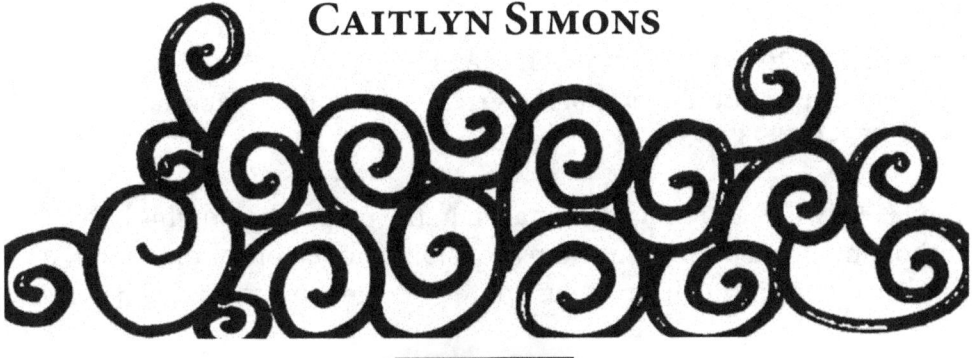

WPR BOOKS: Latino Insights
CARLSBAD, CA

Copyright © 2013 by ALINA GONZALEZ
Printed in the United States of America. All Rights Reserved.
ISBN 978-1-889379-51-7

While every precaution has been taken in the preparation of this book, the author and publisher assume no responsibility for errors or omissions, or for damages resulting from the use of the information contained herein.

For more about books presented by WPR Publishing, please go to www.WPRbooks.com.

Cover illustrations by Caitlyn Simons.

WPR BOOKS: Latino Insights
3445 Catalina Dr., Carlsbad, CA 92010-2856
www.WPRbooks.com   760-434-1223   kirk@whisler.com

Dedications

(2 may 2013)

How
Simple

It is to write
About love,

How difficult it is
To achieve it.

  I could dedicate this to the guys who broke my heart, made me curse myself for sending the first text, and made me realize that there is something better for me out there but I no longer carry them in my heart.

  Emme, this is for you. I know you're still too young to understand the words on these pages but one day you will find love and I will be too old and uncool to aid you during your first heartbreak. So sweetie, take this poetry to heart. A girl always remembers her first love. The way he smiles at you two rows away in English and how he talks loudly about Geometry to try and impress you. While he might seem like the raddest thing since boba tea, he isn't all that great. Trust me. Hold out a little bit longer, have patience and your knight in shinning armor will appear when you least expect him to.

Table of Contents

Dedications — 3
Acknowledgments — 7
Introduction — 8

Illecebrous — 11
    Hola Bonita — 13
    Someplace — 14
    A Dream is a Wish — 16
    Escape — 18
    From A Distance — 20
    Mariposas/Butterflies — 21
    Wishing — 22
    No Idea — 23

Elysian — 25
    Thoughts (24 july 2012) — 27
    Who? — 28
    Different — 30
    Hi. Hello. Good day — 32
    Shy & Seductive — 36
    Simple Things — 38
    Copper Tellurium — 40
    Looking for Alaska — 42
    2 am — 43
    Remind Me — 44

Tristful — 47
    Remember — 49
    Stupid Love — 50
    The Older Guy — 52
    Wrong — 54
    Romeo — 56
    Time — 59
    Unimportant — 60
    No Talking — 61
    Please — 62
    Lies — 62

Sunshine	64
Happy Never After	64

Razbliuto — **67**

Hope (6 august 2012)	69
Having Hope	70
Hope Lies	73
The First Time We Met	74
Unwanted Memories	75
Feelings Subside	76
Natural Disaster	78
Scars (19 august 2012)	80
Sill Loved You	82
November	84
A Last Love Letter	86
Look Away	92
Never Loved You	94
Last Kiss	96
Blaming Myself	98

Trouvaille — **101**

Moving On	103
Content	104
Caught	105
8 months	106
(24 may 2013)	107

Meet the Illustrartor: Caitlyn Simons brief bio	**109**
Meet the Author: Alina Gonzalez brief bio	**110**
WPR Books: Latino Insights	112

Acknowledgements

    I'd first like to thank my inspirations for this book, nine boys who I grew to love during my high school years. You taught me what to look for in the perfect guy and what to definitely avoid. Although you might never read these poems, I just hope you know that at one point in my life you meant the world to me, I just wasn't your world. I'd also like to thank some of my wonderful guy friends who allowed me to use them as models in this book: Josue "Swey" Rodriguez, Daniel Garcia, Jarin Thiem, Joseph Ramirez, Lawrence Kattoula, Shaker Kattoula, Aaron Symes, Fernando Estrada, and Samuel Levi McDaniels. You are all such amazing friends and I couldn't have asked for a greater group of guys to have in my life. To Caitlyn Simons, my beautiful Ginger bestie, thank you for your creativity and willingness to help with the artwork in this book. Macy and Tori, thank you for staying up at odd hours to read my poems and assuring me people will like them. Mamí, gracias for teaching me that writing heals. Thank you for never telling me to put the pen down. Abuelita and Abuelito for setting a positive example of marriage. Isabel Campoy who first told me that a girls poems about love and heartbreak were inspiring and bookworthy and Mr. Whisler for giving me this opportunity. Lastly I'd like to thank you, my reader, I hope that these poems help you remember high school and the first time you fell in love.

Introduction

𝔒𝔫𝔠𝔢 𝔲𝔭𝔬𝔫 𝔞 𝔱𝔦𝔪𝔢, there was a girl who fell hopelessly in love with a boy. She played the game of love very carelessly as she fell into his never-failing charade. He courted her, told her she was beautiful, and even promised her the world. He swore that nothing would ever tear their star-crossed love apart and with each passing day, she fell deeper and deeper in love with him.

They had many good days. Days when they wouldn't go to sleep and talked all night. Days when hugs goodbye lasted a lifetime. Days when silly, childish conversations made her smile. Days when the longing look in his eyes made her blush. Days when she'd wake up to five texts all preparing her for the day. And days when he just had to be him to turn all their time spent into the best part of her day. However, they had bad days too. Nights that she'd cry herself to sleep because of things he said. Nights where she'd analyze and worry about the distance that seemed to appear suddenly, but during these nights, she'd just shake off all the negative feelings because she knew they could get through this.

But, as it is with every fairytale, the hopes of a sudden happy ever after are rarely ever achieved. She soon discovered the truth to his lies: how there was someone else, how he just wanted one thing, how he didn't like her because she was "broken." And all this broke her heart.

She spent more nights than ever crying to numb her broken heart. She swore she'd never find another guy like him and was absolutely positive she would never love again.

She played back memories of the two of them and looked for warning signs of when he stopped loving her. She questioned herself if she ever loved him. She tried talking to him, seeing if they could just be friends; hoping that he would realize he made a mistake and then come back to her. And throughout this whole time, she closed herself off to other love.

It was not until one day that she was in her backyard watching butterflies that she finally understood love. She sat on a tattered blanket and smiled as two simple white butterflies played in the sun; but mid-flight, one butterfly flew away from the other. The abandoned butterfly followed after the first but was always being left. Finally, after so many tries, the lonely butterfly stopped chasing and almost instantly a new, beautiful and brightly colored butterfly approached the abandoned white one and the two set off, dancing off in the sunset.

It was then that the girl understood that something better always comes around, so she stopped her grieving and smiled at the world once again.

Her story of falling in and out love is found on these pages and though she doesn't know what love actually is—she's still fairly young—she is on her way to discovering her new, beautiful and bright butterfly to fly across the sunset with.

illecebrous
(adj.) alluring, attractive, enticing

Picture Provided by Josue Rodriguez

Hola Bonita

My mind's rambled
You seemed like the perfect amigo
I never would be scrambled
For words
To say to you,

But now
After we talked outside of class
And you said,
"Hola bonita,"
I'm confused.
I'm not a chicitita
I know what the word means
And how you intended it to be
But why call me beautiful?
Why me?
Did you mean something? A hidden message in those words?
What did you mean?

I know I shouldn't jump into this
Just because you called me beautiful.
I know you probably didn't mean it,
I mean why would you?
I am not beautiful,
Bonita,
Nope.
No soy nada de eso, I am none of that

And now you made my heart confused
And made me fall in love with you
Just for those two words
That I will never know
If you meant them
Or not.

Someplace

Let's lie awake, side-by-side,
Stare at the stars,
And pretend that
We are far,
Far,
Away from here.

Look past
The sun,
Gaze beyond
The galaxies,
And just get away.

Away from their
Thoughts.
Away from their
Words.
Away from their quidnup ways of being,
And just go someplace,
Where it's just the two of us
And no one else.

SERENDIPITY
BY ALINA GONZALEZ

Somewhere
Where they can't judge us,
Somewhere
Where they can't lie to us,

Somewhere
Where it's no one but us,
Beyond the galaxies,
Past the sun,
Behind the stars,
Somewhere,
Someplace,
Where it's just the two of us, side by side,
Lying awake.

A Dream is A Wish

They say a dream
Is a wish
Your heart makes
And my heart
Has been dreaming
The same dream
Lately….

My heart races
When I think of
Him.

Serendipity
by Alina Gonzalez

Picture Provided by Jarin Thiem

Escape

There's a place
I want to escape to
One that will take
My worries away.
One that is so sweet,
As a single embrace.
One that is so mesmerizing
As the sun as it sets,
And one that continues
To not let my heart rest.

So very few
Can take me there
But I reach my escape
With your questionative glare;

It sails me in an ocean
So endless like your eyes,
Keeps me in a high
Of your voice saying lullabies.
Makes me swim,
In a fit of laughter
When you tell a joke
That I don't get until after;

SERENDIPITY
BY ALINA GONZALEZ

I love my escape
That I get from you
It gives me grace
For the things I haven't said
or the things I do,

But you have no idea
That you take me there,
Make me oblivious in my escape
With your questionative glare.

From a Distance

say hello
just once more.

tell me again
how I sounded like an angel.

laugh a little
to change the subject.

smile once more
to cloud my judgment.

flirt a tad
so I can flirt back.

Leave without a goodbye
So I can pretend
Our conversation
Had no end.

Serendipity
by Alina Gonzalez

Mariposas

Maripositas
Me hinchen la piel
Cuando pienso
En el,

Su sonrisa
Da prisa
A mi Corazon

Y se que el
Me ve solo
Como una amiga
Pero su sonrisa
Me hace rezar
Que se termina
Esa Amistad.

Butterflies

Butterflies
Give me goose bumps
When I think
Of him,

His smile
Makes my
Heart race

I know that he
Sees me
Only as a friend
But when I see his smile
I pray that
The friendship
Will end.

Wishing

In the sleepless nights

I dream of you

In a story of make believe,

Where all is good

And I find you

Beyond a wish

I long to see.

No Idea

Were under the same moon tonight
And you have no idea.
You took my heart at first sight
And you have no idea.
We might wish on the same star tonight
And you have no idea.
I am madly and involuntarily in love with you
And you have no idea.

Elysian
(adj.) beautiful or creative,
divinely inspired; peaceful &
perfect

Picture Provided by Joseph Ramirez

Thoughts (24 july 2012)

If the sun were to crash

Far from the earth,

And the moon refuses to shine

Its light in mirth,

And all the birds stopped in flight

Afraid of the sky,

And all the flowers died

From lack of love,

And the waves turned silent

Alone by themselves,

And the world were to turn gray

From head to toe,

Where would you be love?

Where would you go?

Who?

Hey there
You're so funny
So…
Cute.

Can I tell you a secret?

Lean in a little closer,
You can't tell anyone,
Promise?

Well,
I like this guy-
Who?

Oh, you know him,
He's amazing
Incredible,
So great
He's in your grade too-
Who?
Well he has the best hair
Oh and his eyes,
I could stare at them forever,
But his smile…
That's the part I love the most
It's my favorite and-
Who?
Well he has a class with me
You're in that class too,
So I have an excuse to talk to him-
Who?

Serendipity
by Alina Gonzalez

Oh...
Well can I seriously trust you?
Trust you won't tell?
Cause I don't want things to be awkward
Or hard
Or not go well,
See cause you know him really well,
You know him best of all and-
Who? Who is it?
Oh, well...
It's **you**.

Different

I like you
But you're
Different
Than what I'm used to
What I normally go for.

You seem smart
But it's more…

Your smile
And eyes

That draws me to you
And I'm caught in a trance
When I talk to you.

SERENDIPITY
by Alina Gonzalez

Picture Provided by Shaker Kattoula

Hi, Hello, Good day

Hi
Hello
Good day,
There are so many things,
I'd like to say,
Starting off with a hey
Is much too simple,
But here I struggle for the words,
Trying not to stare,
Trying not to give it away,
Trying to find the strength inside
Me.

You're beautiful,
And I like
You...

There I said it,
Said the words out loud
Words that could break and ruin me,
Words that could make and build you,
Because it's all up to you now
It's all you,

SERENDIPITY
BY ALINA GONZALEZ

You're the decider of my path
The chooser of the one I take
A trail of happiness.

A road of loneliness.
All leading to a bigger
Me,
More beautiful
You.

So what is your choice?
Do you love me too?
Do you even know my name?
Know what you do to me?
Taking my breath away
Making me count the days,
Until I see you again.
Do you realize,
How much you've made me care,
How much you've opened my eyes?
How much joy you cause me,
And how much pain?

I love you.
I've said it.
No turning back now,
No friendship from love,

No love to friendship.

I've set myself free,
And placed me into your misery,
You are whom I care for,
Whom I adore
And want to love.

I've said it now,
And please,
Don't tear my heart,
I blinded myself,
For I already know,
How you feel,
But I had hope,
That that would change,
Hope things could be rearranged,
The cards have been played,
The ball's in your court,
It up to you to choose.

Please,
I've said it now.
I've said those words.
Words that will cause me hurt,
Pain,
Words that I cannot take back,
They are no longer just in my head,
They linger in this open air,

Serendipity
by Alina Gonzalez

Everywhere.
My words.
Those words.

Aren't private anymore,
No longer are they secure,
The whole wide world
Sees them written outside
My door,
Those words were not
God-forbidden,
Not undeniable,
Not wrong...

Those words were not wrong,
Yet they feel that way,
To the contrary
They were suppose to feel right,
But no.
I've said those words
There's no turning back. No.
I've said those words,
Out loud.
I've said those words,
Broken the barriers.
I've said those words,
When all I was trying to say was

"hi..."

Shy & Seductive

I don't
Understand you sometimes.

You can be so
Seductive with your concentrated
Look when working
In class,

Yet so shy
With your hands on me and
Your wink and your smile.

And I don't know how to
Tell you
That it drives me

Crazy.

SERENDIPITY
BY ALINA GONZALEZ

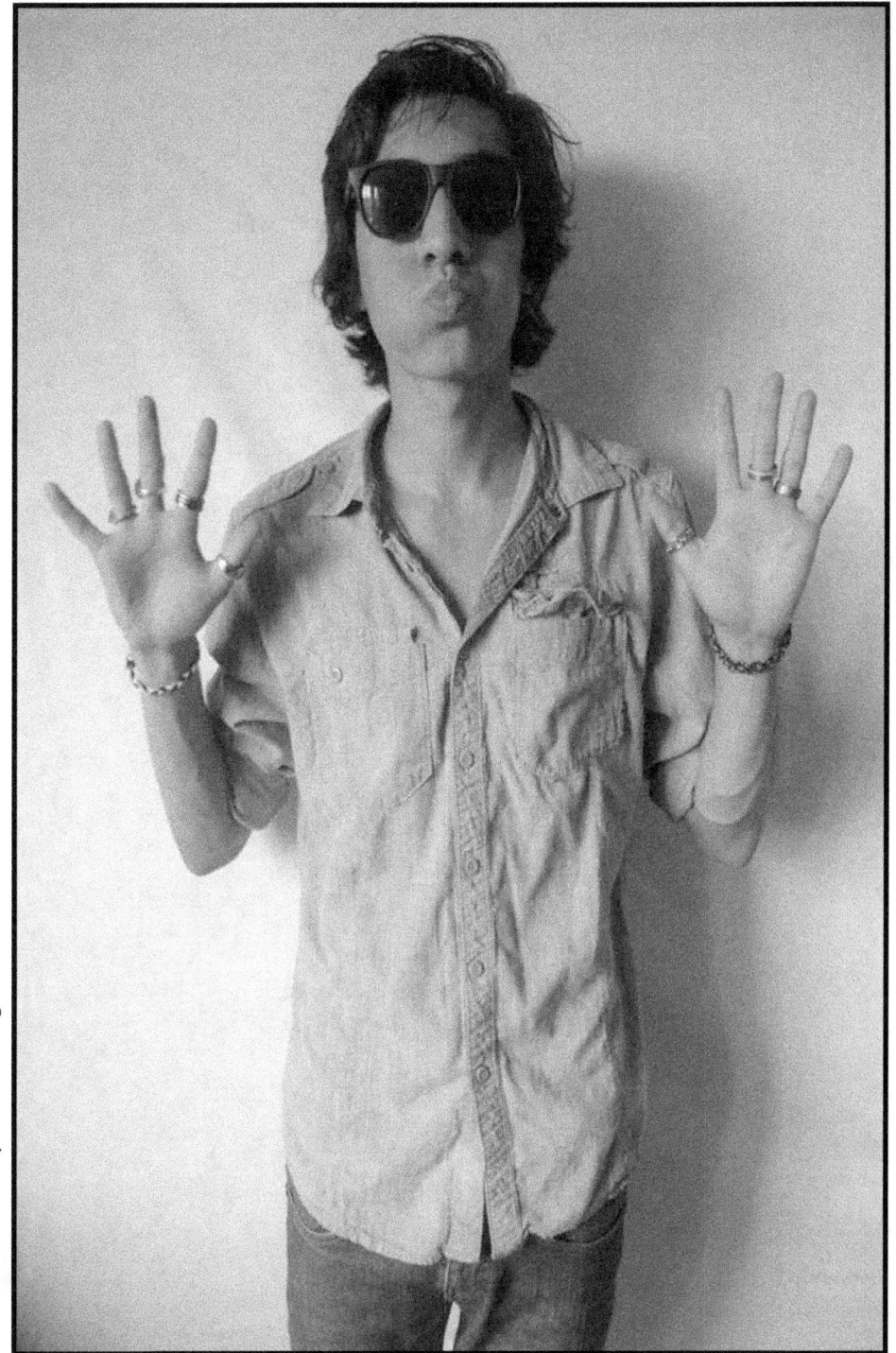

Picture Provided by Josue Rodriguez

Simple Things

We were standing so close,
With the comfort of your arm on me.
I could close my eyes
And you wouldn't disappear.
I believed you'd stay there
Just for me.

So we laughed a bit,
Giggled at the most nonsensical of things
Just to hear each other,
Just to be close.

And we repeated words,
"I'm sorry"
And
"I love you."
Only when I said the latter,
You probably didn't understand.

Sure we were just saying
What they wanted us to say,
But I meant something more
And I think you knew,

Because you glanced my way
And leaned a little more in
Squeezing my arm
Placing me near
Your face…

SERENDIPITY
BY ALINA GONZALEZ

But I drew my breath.
Laughed it off.
You did too.
But your voice was soft
When you said
"____, I love you."
And I replied
"I love you too, ____."

And you just looked at me
And smiled.
And I smiled back .
And time passed
As we kept sneaking glances
At each other,
Realizing that life
Can be so perfect at times
In the most simple moments,
In the most innocent of times.

And time passed.
We laughed.
We smiled
As time passed,
Showing
That perfect
Can be in the most
Simple of things.

Copper Tellurium

Darkness,
Stars,
The light in your eyes...

I wanted to tell you then
As we spoke of chemistry
With all the world around us--
But none of it touching us--
Because I'm transfixed by your eyes.

Of course I can't let you know,
Cause then your mind would change.
Maybe.
I'm not too sure.

So we just continue
I sit and
You stand
Making me laugh and smile
Letting me forget everything
For a while.

I like this..
It feels natural
And right.
Nothing forced
And nothing hidden,
And because nothing was hidden
I told you;

SERENDIPITY
BY ALINA GONZALEZ

I didn't want to seem like
I was a flirt,
But I was toying with your friend when I saw you
And then there was that familiar pang in my chest
As I noticed the gleam of your eyes--
The questionable look.
But I shrugged it off
Because I had already led on your friend,
And I didn't want to feel bad;

But as we got to know each other
I turned my back to your friend.
You never questioned it.
But you must have wanted to know why.

So in the darkness
Under the stars
I made you guess what I first thought of you
And when you were close
I said let's go back to chemistry--
Just to stay on the safe side.
But we brought chemistry into it,
And that how we ended up with
Copper Tellurium.

And we were both such nerds,
That that was the best way to put it.

Looking for Alaska

I read an entire book--

One of your favorites--

All in one night,

Just so that we could have

Something to talk about

The next day.

2 am

I thought about you
One time at
2 am
when all the world
was asleep
and my mind longed to be awake
so that it could
vividly picture your face.

And in the silence
At 2 am
My heart longed for you
And it wondered
Who yours longed for
Too.

Remind Me

It's funny how
Simple things
Remind me of you…

Like the ring on my pinky
With its turquoise stone
And how you saw it
Then showed me your belt buckle
With its turquoise stone
That had belonged to your father;

Or my light blue nail polish
That I repainted once
Because you didn't like the
Silver glitter on it;

Or my left hand
Which you held sweetly
The time we talked about college
And you asked what I had
In mind,
Never letting go
Until someone asked why
We were holding hands
And you slowly untangled
Your fingers from mine;

Or how clear and beautiful
And endless
Your eyes looked
That brief moment we stared
Into each others;

SERENDIPITY
BY ALINA GONZALEZ

Or the way you pat my
Arm
And cheek
And head
And how you cup my face
And slyly
And unintentionally
Reach your arm over and touch
My arm,
Face,
Leg
Without looking;

Or how your sarcasm
Translates
Into your texts
And I can easily imagine
How you would say it;

Or how *Part of Your World*,
When Will My Life Begin,
And *Hello*
All now remind me of you;

Or how when I make
That face
Where I scrunch up my
Lips to one corner of my mouth
I can picture you imitating me
And asking, again,
Why I make that face.

Yes,
Little, simple things
Remind me of
You.

Tristful
(adj.) deeply yet romantically melancholy.

Tristful

Remember

I remember you
And you remember me,
All the good times we shared,
All the memories
And now you're back
From your hideaway place,
Ready to put
A smile on my face.

You remember all my jokes,
I remember all your stories
The boys I used to like
And the girls you saw
Before me.

But I remember you
And you remember me
And we both remember
How happy the two of us

Used to be.

Stupid Love

I've spent quite a bit of time
Just sitting on the sidelines,
Watching silently
As arrows would strike
And people would fall
For each other.

I was glad it wasn't happening to me.
I was able to just run around
However I pleased;
It was all too perfect,
For too long.

Lying in bed
Cursing myself again
Knowing that I shouldn't have sent
The message I sent.

It's pretty late.
Yet I can't sleep
Cause I'm too busy
Thinking about you...

I don't want to like you,
Yet I do.

SERENDIPITY
BY ALINA GONZALEZ

I'm not really sure
What attracts me to you;
You're smart and kind,
Sweet and funny,
A total dork,
And a little awkward.

But I'm just hoping
You're ok
With my silence and smiles
And unnecessary words
And how tongue tied I get
When you look my way.

Yet, maybe you hardly notice
And that's why you haven't replied
So I stay here and lay down,
Cursing myself with my phone
By my side.

The Older Guy

I met someone
And he seems amazing...
But I barely know him...
He's older too,
So none of my friends approve
But he somehow manages
To take my breath away....

He's a freshman
And I am too,
But at completely different schools.
It's a four-year difference
And it's not that much
Yet to everyone
It seems to be.

I can't imagine him
Meaning to purposely
Hurt me
Or force me into something
I don't want to do.

He seems way too sweet,
Way too nice
But sometimes I wonder...

Is it all a disguise?
Are the words my friends say true?
Are those things
He'd really do?

SERENDIPITY
BY ALINA GONZALEZ

I can't imagine it
Picture it
Think of it
He doesn't seem like that kind of guy
He seems...
Kind
Shy
Quiet
Smart
A little dorky...
So if that's how he seems
Then he wouldn't do those things...

Right?

Wrong

Could I just say something?
It'll only take a moment,
I came across a problem
And I thought I should point it
Out.

You see,
It's amazing how
You're into me
But is it really
Wise?

You're way older
And I'm so young,
People will say things,
Say you just want fun
And whisper
Words.

They'll say words,
Just wanting to
Be heard,
And try to convince me
That this is
Wrong.

I don't want them to think,
That you're something
You're not,
To judge the way you seem,
Because they're
Wrong.

Serendipity
by Alina Gonzalez

Romeo

I asked you
To be my Romeo,
You said you'd
Love to,
And you're good
With a kiss,
I thought you were
Obnoxious,
And a goober
But I also thought,
It was cute,
And I liked you.

But you're a Montague,
In your college palace,
And I a Capulet,
In my childish world
And there is no way
That we could be together.

Serendipity
by Alina Gonzalez

My parents don't approve,
Society doesn't want me
To like you.
No one thinks
That you should be
My Romeo,
That there shouldn't be
A tragic ending with one final kiss,
No eloping
In nonsense,
No happiness,
Just strict
Honor to my name.

But I love you,
My Romeo,
And I'd drink a poison
To be with you,
To run away
From society's
Feud;
To be happy
Sealed in happiness
With a kiss,
Being your Juliet
And taking off
To view the world
Together,

Ignoring that it's
Our love
That they try
To weather.

I want you
And only you
To be my prince,
Blinded by love
In a cheery
Bliss,
Drink the poison
Without thinking,
Just to kiss your lips
And have you
Be,
My Romeo.

SERENDIPITY
BY ALINA GONZALEZ

Time

I feel like painting,
But my hands won't hold the brush.

I feel like writing,
But all my words turn to mush.

I feel like talking on the phone,
But no number comes mind.

I feel like sleeping
Until I've broken the concept of time.

Unimportant

When you love
Someone
And make them
A part of you
It hurts so much to let them
Leave,

But you were toxic
And I fell for it
Because you acted
Like you wanted
Me.

I fell for every
Word you said,
Every touch, every glance,
I fell for it
All.

I know how
Angry I must
Sound
But you took away
A part of me
I hadn't even found.

I'm sorry I let you do that.
I'm sorry I let you believe
You were that important
To me.

No Talking

I'm kind of really sad that
We don't talk
Anomore.

I don't really
Have anyone I can trust a
s much as I trusted
You.

No one who
Will really listen
To my stories of when I think
I'm in love.

No one to stay up with me all night
So the dark voices
Don't take my life.

I really have
No one
Who will understand me
Like you did.

And, although
I crave to talk to you,
I hold back.

So that,
After 30 messages,
You don't have to feel the need to apologize
For ignoring
Me

And then doing it
Once again.

Please

Don't just stand there
Acting like you care.

Let me go
So I can breath the
Open air.

Lies

Tell me how beautiful I am.

Lie to me
I know you can.

SERENDIPITY
by Alina Gonzalez

Picture Provided by Daniel Garcia

Sunshine

I really want to text you

Because you said I could

Anytime I felt...bad again

And you'd be there to talk and listen...

But I don't know how

And I don't want to bother you

So I call up other guys

Who have broken my heart more than you have

And I try to fill this void

And I sit in my room

And paint a giant sun on my wall

So I can have something bright to contrast my thoughts

And I want to text you

Cuz you always make me smile

But I'm most likely the farthest thing on your mind

So I stare at my wall

Hoping the sun will warm me up inside.

SERENDIPITY
BY ALINA GONZALEZ

Happy Never After

Stars fall

Twinkling in the sky.

Tears drop

Of memories of you and I.

What happened to

All the fairy tales

Of used-to-be's?

The magical sparks

And daydreams?

Razbliuto

(n.) the sentimental feeling you have about someone you onced loved but no longer do.

Picture Provided by Lawrence Kattuola

Serendipity
by Alina Gonzalez

Hope (6 august 2012)

Once upon a time

I met you

And then there were butterflies.

And lies.

And cries.

And hope.

But you didn't bring the lies

Or the tears.

Hope did.

And hope is my greatest fear.

Having Hope

So,
By chance,
I met you.
And from that day on
I grew to fall head over heels
For your smile
And words
And dorkiness
And realness...
But as I fell
I was too clumsy to even note
If you'd be there to catch me,
And once I saw you weren't,
I was already too far down the way
And could not fly away.

So I waited
And watched
And wondered,
If I could ever be who you'd want,
I tried to make myself open,
Approachable,
Perfect,
But I had to look past to see that that was more than you could be
So it wasn't what you could be with...

SERENDIPITY
BY ALINA GONZALEZ

And after some truth
I let you see
Just how vulnerable I used to be,
And you said you understood.

But you didn't.

I wasn't just another girl in your charades of flirtations,
I wasn't just someone you could dispose of,
I wasn't another fan of your looks,
Or awestruck by your smile,
Or swooning over your physical qualities,
And that was what you understood...

You don't know what I am,
All you know is that
It's too much for you.

So our phone calls and texts grew to extinction
And you let me sit here
Like a dork
Waiting for a reply
That will never come....

You knew I would play your game,
At least you thought you did.
You knew I was smart,
But smart enough to crack your puzzle?

Razbliuto

No.

But I've had many experiences
And broken trusts
And lies
To not be so delicate.
I now how to be strong
And not give in
So easily-- even if it looks like I do.
I know just when to give up,
I know when the indignant one doesn't like you back.

You thought my flaw and weakness was you--
They all think that.

But it's not.

It's deeper than that
And it crushes me,
Because my biggest flaw
Is having hope
That one day
There'll be a
You and me.

Hope Lies

It lasted three days.

The whimsical butterflies,
The racing pulse of my heart,
The look in my eyes,
The craving when you were apart from me...

In its entirety
I knew the truth
But it was something I just refused
To accept because I had hope.

But hope doesn't transfer into love,
It translates into broken hearts
And dead emptiness
And lonely nights.
Hope isn't lovely.

But in those three days
Hope kept me alive,
Kept some light in me,
Some chance I could believe
I'd no longer just be the friend...

But hope lies.

The First Time We Met

The night,
It was dark,
We had something in common
We played a few games.

You sat by me
In darkness
Smiling until you
Realized I was taken
And innocently said
It's ok to have feelings for
Another,
Even if you have a significant one.

But that innocent smile,
Was a devilish grin
When you caught on
How easy
My heart

Could

Give

In.

Serendipity
by Alina Gonzalez

Unwanted Memories

I remember the way you looked at me
That night we spent watching movies,
How you burnt yourself
Baking brownies,

And how you ran to me
For a quick kiss.

All these memories make me smile
Yet, make me so sad…

The way you'd say, "Hello gorgeous?"
When I'd call,

And the sound of you riding
Your bike home,

How your eyes lit up
When I showed you something new,

I crave these memories
And so many more,

But I still just want
To forget you.

Feelings Subside

I don't like you.
I don't.

So why do you
Continue to make my heart
Race
Leave me blinded
Caught in the embrace
Of your eyes.
Why are you making this difficult?
I keep coming back
But why?

Stop smiling at me,
Remembering my favorite color,
Winking,
And trying to create
Inside things.
Why must you tease me?
And not talk to me later?
I'm too stupid
When you give me
The time of day,
Undeserving of a beautiful bouquet.

You don't like me.
You don't.

SERENDIPITY
BY ALINA GONZALEZ

So stop confusing me.
Getting on your knees.
Smiling.
Taunting me to believe
You still do.
Just let me go
So I can let go
And stop returning
Back to you.

I won't say I love you.
I won't.

Because then you'd have accomplish
What you were here to do
I'm not giving my heart to you
I'm subsiding the feeling
Hiding the crazed me
That keeps on believing
You love me too.

So don't look my way
Don't talk to me today
Don't smile
Or think.
Or try to reach me.
I won't answer.
Won't pick up.
I'll be dying inside.
But I'll just let the feelings
subside.

Natural Disaster

I wanted to
Play it safe
Not worrying bout
A real chase
Or a real deal
With love and kisses
And fake fate.

I thought I had
My ducks in a row
That nothing would
Shatter
With one single blow,

Until the quake
Of realization arrived
I thought I had convinced
Myself with my own disguise.

The fire burns
It shakes and quivers,

Serendipity
by Alina Gonzalez

My knees give out
My heart races
Round
As my mind paces
The foreground
My palms become to shallow seas
My eyes adjust to only see
You.

I'm trapped in a disaster
Falling faster.
    And faster.
        And faster.
Going until
I'm gone
Moving fast
Along.
Trying to say I love you,
Actually saying goodbye.

I'm gone,
    Away,
        Far away,
For the mistake
Of loving
A natural disaster.

Scars (19 august 2012)

So we sat in the dark,
Heart beats in one,
I knew I shouldn't have but I still did.

I longed to talk to you,
To feel your arms around me,
Once we were like that,
I didn't want it to end,
Nothing else was there,
Just you and me,
And I never wanted to let go….

I remember our last hug like that,
The one where I kissed you…
You were shocked
And I smiled
Then you did too,
I've missed that
Just how I've missed you.

SERENDIPITY
BY ALINA GONZALEZ

So in that darkness
When we talked,
We learned new things
And you looked at me
With new eyes,

You looked down and sad when I told you,
Then pulled out a flashlight and asked to see my scars,
You gently grasped my arm and searched for them,
Brought them close to your face as if you were going to kiss them,
But then you looked away....

I know we've changed
We've both said words,
But are we really that far apart?

I miss you
I know you miss us too,

> But I feel like that hug
> Was the last of you
> and me.

Still Loved You

I'm not sure that I can

Trust someone

As much as I did you.

You were incredible in

Some ways,

But extremely horrible

In others.

But I,

For some reason,

Still loved you.

SERENDIPITY
by Alina Gonzalez

Picture provided by Fernando Estrada

November

It's been a year since you told me,
Do you realize it too?
Do you remember?
It was that one-day in November,
When we talked about
Love
And how I believed it's a fairytale
And how you saw it as a lie.

How emotions are overrated
And that love can be outdated,
But just as we talked bout how your perfect girl would be
I said I had a perfect guy in mind
And you asked,

"Is it me?"

I couldn't believe my eyes,
I reread that text
Millions if times,
My heart would skip a beat
And that was how I knew
You loved me too.

SERENDIPITY
BY ALINA GONZALEZ

But the year has gone
It seems like we've both moved on,
But I haven't completely,
Have you?

I see your happiness
With other girls,
And you say you have,
I say I have too,
But I always come back to that day,
Will I ever move on?
Do you ever remember,
That night in November?

We could have been more.

But now we've gone
Our separate ways.

A Last Love Letter

Dearest ____,

I know I must be too late,
I was too late a long time ago as well,
But you must know...

I love you.

It's rude to say
And I know you probably no longer care
But I do.

It's hard to see you now,
We hardly talk
And we can be in the same room
Five feet from each other
And not say a word,
Not even a glance in the others direction....

When you told me
My whole world stopped.

I wanted to cry-
I did cry.

Serendipity
by Alina Gonzalez

I can't stand to see you with her.
That's all wrong.

It's not right.

We never even got a chance.

I thought we'd have forever
So I kept saying no.

Do you really love her?
Or are you just playing along
With their dumb charade?

Don't waste your life,
Please.

Don't throw away 5 years...

I can't even look at you anymore,
Who are you?
We're strangers
And to you it's ok.

It's ok for you to know I'm not really happy for you,
It's ok to see me hide behind a smile,
It's ok to leave with empty words
And unmade, already broken promises.

Razbliuto

It's ok....

I love you, ____.
I always have
And I always will.

I don't understand why you'd rather be with her
But maybe I'm not suppose to...

I guess what we are is many things...

We are the cracked, dead leaves falling from dry branches,
We are the stars crashing down in space,
We are the broken pieces of a deserted path,
We are gone.

We are so many things,
But not at all what I wished we could be.

We are gone
And we are dead.

I don't want to see us die anymore.

I don't want us in each other's lives anymore.

Serendipity
by Alina Gonzalez

We've already had our goodbyes
And there's no way we can mend,

> Just know
> I love you,

I've loved you since that day you offered to tutor me in science
And I said yes, even though I had a higher grade than you.

I've loved you since you sat by me in the spelling bee
And purposely messed up a word because I told you I wanted to win.

I've loved you since I walked away from you
And you called after me apologizing and calling me back.

I've loved since we stood next to each other after the play
And you apologized for something stupid you had done.

I've loved you since we had a late night text conversation
And you told me you were better than my dream guy.

I've loved you since you took three days to tell me that you liked me
And you even called it *love*.

I've loved you since we passed that note asking if we loved each other
And you said your mind was confused but your heart said yes.

I've loved you since we had that huge fight
And I swore I'd never talk to you again.

Razbliuto

I've loved you since you asked if we could start over

And you said, "hi my name is ____."

I've loved you since we wrote mini novels inside each other's yearbooks
And you told me you loved talking to me.

I've loved you since you forgot all by birthdays
But woke me up at midnight one year and told me you were thinking about me and happy birthday.

I've loved you since I would pass you notes
And you told me you've saved every note and letter I've ever given you.

I will always love you, _____,
And I wish you the best in life.

With all my heart,
_____

SERENDIPITY
BY ALINA GONZALEZ

Picture provided by Shaker Kattuola

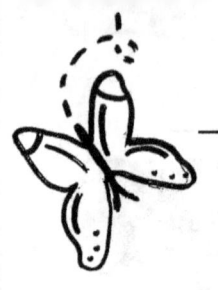

Look Away

It's been a year,
365 days since an end,
Where darkness came over me
From the snap of a tiny lie...

False words were said
And warm smiles exchanged
Heat spread
At the gasp of your name...

Dark shadows
Arms twined
Searching for your lips
Yours reaching mine...

Building up hopes
Breaking down dreams
Unleashing something deep
Inside of me...

Longing to see you again
Remembering the feel of you against me
The way you whispered and pulled me close...

Recalling empty theatres,
Secret corners
Quick and anxious kisses,
Silent exchanges...

SERENDIPITY
BY ALINA GONZALEZ

The way you'd look at me and say my name
Try to make me fall into your boyish game...

And I fell fast
Wanting you to want me
To crave a kiss like I did
To feel how I felt when you touched me
To be the one you'd hide away with...

And now after a year
After thoughts and memories
After tears and internal fights
After hurt and pain
After a year of regrets
I might see you again...

I might look up at the face
That once made my heart stop,
The smile that once gave me goose bumps
That gaze that once made me speechless
The boy who I once thought was a man...

After a year of waiting for an explanation why
I know if we meet again
You'll only do the same as I
You'll look away
Not ever asking
Once
If I was ever okay...

Never Loved You

I trusted you,
I let you see
Deep down inside of me,
I opened up
More than ever before,
And in an instant
I crushed the glass
To the floor;
I broke and shattered,
Every last thread
Of hope and happiness
Saying the words I said.

I never truly loved you,
It's painful to say
But you were just there at the
Wrong time,
On the wrong day.

I was vulnerable
And weak.

SERENDIPITY
BY ALINA GONZALEZ

You lifted me up,
Made me create
A vision of love and lust,
But I never loved you.
Nope.

Not one bit.
You were just something to make me forget,
Someone who said words that meant
That I was good
Not bad.
You told me what
I wanted to hear.
You said you'd love me forever
And ever.
I feared
You might mean it,
And I didn't want that.
So I looked away
And said
Enough is enough.
And I ended it.
Just like that.

I ended it,
Just like that.

Last Kiss

Do you remember
Our last kiss?

I do.

We were standing by the side of the house.
Desperately and achingly
You pulled me in
And I laughed
And you smiled
As our lips met for the kiss…

I pulled away,
Thinking this was our normal,
Quick kiss goodbye
But with your arms around my waist
You pulled me in
Closer…

Begging to keep my hands tangled
In your messy, black hair
Moving your hand to my face,
Cupping my cheek,
You pulled me in
Urging the kiss not to end….

SERENDIPITY
BY ALINA GONZALEZ

I remember how
Confused I was,
You had never kissed me this way before,
And all this I thought
As you pulled me in.
And at that moment I knew
This relationship would change…

We had promised that
Neither of us would
Get emotionally attached

We didn't want the pain,

We had said that
It was all
Just for fun,

So not to worry that one-day

One of us might
Fall in love…

Though you didn't tell me,
That kiss
Was all you had to
Say.

Blaming Myself

I can't remember why I fell in love with you.

You should have just
Stayed out of my way
And not have said a thing
When I asked if you wanted to play,

But across that chessboard
You smiled this most *beautiful*
And evil smile
A smile I couldn't resist—so wonderful,

You called me beautiful
That's all I needed to hear
From then on you had me
I fell in love with no fear,

You liked to show everyone
That I was yours
As if I was some prize you'd won
You walked with your arm around me,

Sneaking me into empty corners for a kiss
Your mouth on mine was pure magic
Your lips were a bliss
That fogged up me reality,

SERENDIPITY
BY ALINA GONZALEZ

You smiled and made everything right
Kiss by kiss
I never put up a fight
For you to win me over, I made it so easy.

And then the darkness turned to gray
And your loving embraced went away
I told you no over and over again
But you did it anyway,

I fought until I gave up
Because no matter how loud I screamed,
no matter the tears I cried,
You only cared about yourself,

When it was over you just left me there
Broken
Laying down with tear stained cheeks and a confused mind
What did I do to make you do that?

I loved you
And you used me for your own gain,
Your own selfish pleasure,
Another girl on your list.

I can't remember why I fell in love with you,
But I know exactly the moment when I stopped loving you.

Trouvaille
(n.) something lovely discovered by chance, a windfall

Picture Provided by Samuel Levi McDaniels

Moving On

Some days I just want to wake up

Look out my window

And know

That there's someone out there

Doing the same

Wondering if

Anyone is doing the same thing

And thinking about them….

Content

Flirty words,
Sly smiles.

At first
It was just for fun.
A game of sorts,
But now…

It's a highlight in my day.
It's a smile to look forward to.
It's time well spent.

It's magical.

And makes me
Oh so
Content.

Caught

I didn't plan on knowing you
You were just this face that was sitting;
This total surprise that
Caught me off-guard….

You were cute
But I'm sort of,
Kind of,
A little too nervous
To talk to you.

So I'm falling back
Into a scheme
Of pitter pattering hearts.

I wasn't prepared
But I'll give it a shot
And then you might just be
Another name that
My broken heart
Caught.

8 months

So I tried a new thing one day
Believing that it'd just be a carefree deal
Not imagining anything
real
To come out of it.

And well,
You were this sudden
Rustle in the leaves
And full of a
Bright smile
That I couldn't believe
I'd stumbled across;
A small prize with my luck
And a
hope
I'd abandoned so long ago.

Lost in the gleam of your eyes
And shaken awake
By the sweet lullaby of your voice
I understood then why it had taken
8 months
To get over a false hope of love,
8 months
To find a heart worth waiting for.

(24 may 2013)

You gave me a

Reason

To write again,

Thank you.

Meet the Illustrator

Caitlyn Simons spends most of her time playing basketball, relaxing with her cat, and working on art. This is her debut as an illustrator. She has entered some pieces in the San Diego county fair in her past years of high school. Aside from illustration, she also excels at photography. While art is one of her passions, Caitlyn plans on attending a Nursing program following her high school graduation this June.

Meet the Author

As this book is completed, Alina Gonzalez is in her Senior year at Valley Center High School in rural San Diego County. *Serendipity* is her first book and is compiled of poetry she wrote during her four years of high school about her various crushes and cute guys.

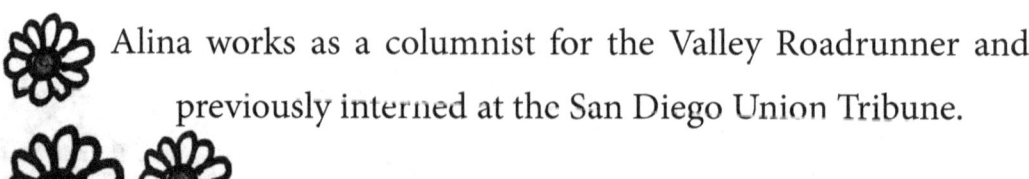

Alina works as a columnist for the Valley Roadrunner and previously interned at the San Diego Union Tribune.

Born with a philanthropic mindset, she believes there is no greater joy than helping someone who could never repay you and actively participates as a volunteer with a number of organizations.

While she is fond of writing, Alina is very passionate in all areas of the arts. Her love for the stage led her to be inducted into the International Thespian Society Troupe #6199 where she avidly participates in theatre productions and competitions with her school's drama program.

Musically inclined, Alina picked up the string bass eight years ago and plays with the San Diego Civic Youth Orchestra's Symphony. In the area of film she has won many awards for directing, editing, writing, and acting in her own self-produced screenplays. She aspires to pursue a career in screenplay writing.

Alina will be attending film school the fall of 2014.

WPR BOOKS
is dedicated to improving protrayals and expanding opportunities for Latinos in the USA

WPR BOOKS has been publishing books and directories since 1983. WPR Books has seven imprints: *Comida, Helping Hands, Heroes, Latino Insights, Latin American Insights, Para los Niños,* and *Total Success.*

Latino Print Network, WPR BOOKS sister organization, works with 625+ Hispanic newspapers and magazines. These publications have a combined circulation of 19 million in 177 markets nationwide. **To stay in touch with sign,** subscribe to our free newsletter at **www.HM101.com**

FOR OUR YOUTH FROM OUR PARA LOS NIÑOS IMPRINT

The Realities of Living in the 21st Century Series is designed to help youth better understand and appreciate the social, health and political issues that many youth face

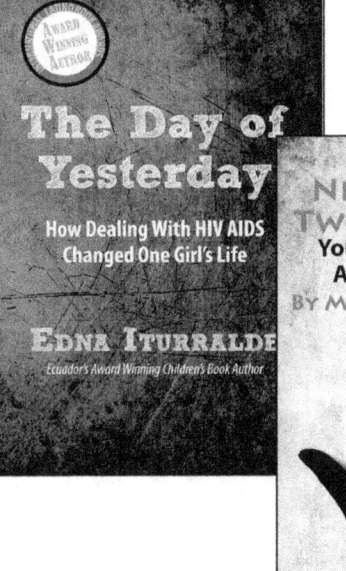

We're adding more books every month

www.ingramcontent.com/pod-product-compliance
Lightning Source LLC
Chambersburg PA
CBHW071400080526
44587CB00017B/3144